"Always respect the Elders because their wisdom comes from the Creator of this Earth."

Dorothy Doolan – Nis'ga
Born 1916, Canyon City, Nass River, B.C.

OUR ELDERS SPEAK

> *"Teach your children what we have taught our children — that the Earth is our Mother."*
>
> — Chief Seattle, 1854

OUR ELDERS SPEAK

A TRIBUTE TO NATIVE ELDERS

Karie Garnier

– VOLUME ONE –

Canadian Cataloguing in Publication Data

Garnier Karie, 1947 –
   Our elders speak

   ISBN0-9695047-0-5

1. Indians of North America-Canada-Portraits
2. Indians of North America-Canada-Quotations
I. Title
E89.G37 1990   971'.00497   C91-091050-2

Earth photo by permission NASA
Printing: Hemlock Printers Ltd., Burnaby, B.C.
Binding: Northwest Bindery, Surrey, B.C.

Photographer, Designer: Karie Garnier

This publication was made possible with the financial assistance of
David Cadman and The United Nations Association of Canada.

Published by: Karie Garnier
                Box 333, 15087 16th Avenue
                White Rock, British Columbia
                Canada   V4A 6G3

To my mother Ferne and Rolling Thunder

Foreword

by Elder Napoleon Kruger

You don't have to be a highly educated person to understand the simple truths that our Elders are speaking about. For there is much wisdom in the few words that each of our Elders speak.

The Mother Earth is the root of this project. And if the cries from the environment are not heeded we could end up with more disease because the land will become depleted of the healthy things that are in it. Many natural medicines are being destroyed. And the destruction across the land has left us with acid rain, contaminated water and foul air.

Many of these things that are happening today were predicted by the Elders a long time ago. And our living Elders are now repeating the prophecies of those Elders who have passed on to the Spirit World.

And like myself, I would not say anything like this if I had not already heard it from my Elders.

Indigenous people in other lands understand the same things that our Elders here have seen, heard, and spoken of. I know this to be true because I have heard this from my Elder Thomas Banyacya, the Hopi prophet who has travelled throughout many countries. Thomas was asked by his Elders to deliver the Hopi prophecies to the world. He did not just get up and do this on his own.

Indigenous Elders around the world teach a fundamental love and respect for all living things. This is why *Our Elders Speak* is an appropriate title for this global project and book on Indigenous Elders.

The more *Our Elders Speak* project increases the global contact with the old ones, and brings out their teachings, I am sure that more people will be blessed with a healthier, more natural focus in their lifestyle. Because people tend to forget the simplicity and the beauty of life on Mother Earth.

And if we don't help take care of our Mother Earth, her sacred waters, and pure air, there will be more sickness spreading throughout the land. I have said this before and I'll say it again because my Elders have told me so.

Sometimes our Elders would speak only once of the sacred things, the mysteries, or what is about to happen. For it is often a God-given message that comes through our Elders. This is why our Elders are saying, "Listen! Listen! Listen when we are speaking. For we may be able to speak this only once!" And as

Elders, we may be allowed to speak once again, but only if our Creator lets us live another day.

But when the big dollar sign speaks it says, "We can forget about our old people and Mother Earth because if we just bulldoze one more road through here, we can cut down all those trees over there, and we can make a lot of fast money." The big dollar is the root of a lot of evil things.

Our Native peoples lived in harmony with nature and the Creator for thousands of years. But a non-Native culture was brought over here saying that our spirituality had no value. Our ancestors told us that only when we return to our spirituality and respect for nature will we find our health and balance with Mother Earth.

Our Elders and Medicine People are still in communion with nature and the Great Spirit. And when an Elder speaks it is sometimes a blessing from our good Creator. This is why many of our young people are coming back to the teachings of the Elders.

If all people, world-wide, will look up, listen to, and respect their Elders then many wonderful things and natural healings will start to happen once again. This we know from our teachings. And this is why I feel so strongly that *Our Elders Speak* is both a timely project and a vitally important piece of literature.

Napoleon Kruger, 1990
Marron Valley, British Columbia

From 1982 to the present I had the honour of visiting more than 70 Elders of the First Native Nations on reserved lands in Western Canada and the United States, recording on film and in print their images and thoughts. *Our Elders Speak* is a photographic tribute to some of these Elders.

The Vision Quest and the Vision

This book evolved through my close association with the First Nations community. It began with the healing of my long illness through indigenous spirituality in 1982. This, in turn, led to a "vision quest" (a solo fast on a mountain under the guidance of the Elders) in 1983: my search for ways to express my new knowledge of the First People. While on the four-day fast at that sacred spot, my feelings of gratitude deepened and the vision became clear: to create a photographic tribute to bring the uplifting wisdom of the Elders to the Canadian public and to the rest of the world. My target was Expo '86.

I began photographing and recording the Elders in 1982. In 1985 the Canada Council Explorations Program awarded me a subsistence grant to help complete the photographic tribute in time for Expo '86. Seven bald eagles soared high over my seaside home the day the Canada Council jury approved my application for the Elder's project.

A Feast for the Elders

Late in 1985, with the world exposition just a few months away and many more Elders to photograph, I was worried that the project was not developing fast enough. Eventually an Elder of the Okanagan Nation advised me to bring the others together in the traditional way. With the help of my family and Native friends, I gave a feast (or potlatch) on November 11, 1985 at the Musqueam Reserve in Vancouver. More than 70 Elders and others, making a total of 100 guests, came from reserved lands and other areas as far away as Squamish, North Vancouver, Chehalis, Sardis, Seabird Island, Hope and Penticton, B.C. We dined on foods of the four seasons — deer meats, bitter roots, wild berries, salmon delicacies — and every Elder was given a personal gift. My family also presented the eldest Elders with a traditional gift of blankets.

Following the dinner and the presentations I felt honoured to stand before the gathering of Elders to speak. I asked them to reflect back over their life and, in the weeks ahead, find their own words for their individual messages which, along with their photographs, would welcome the visitors from around the world at Expo '86. Good feelings filled the hall, as one by one, many Elders stood and voiced their blessings for the photographic project.

Over the following months and years I visited these people in their homes and at Elders' gatherings. I was always warmly received and felt privileged to photograph those Elders delegated by band councils and record their stories and advice in their own words.

Our Elders Speak at Expo '86

I am grateful to The Professional Native Womens' Association who sponsored the completion of the 1986 phase of the project. The Department of the Secretary of State and other organizations also provided financial assistance. The highlight for me was seeing the cavalcade of VIP vehicles and luxury limousines drive out to the reserved lands, pick up all the Elders, and escort them onto the Expo '86 site for the opening ceremonies and the unveiling of the photographic show. The powerful result, *Our Elders Speak, A Tribute To Native Elders* opened the eyes and touched the hearts of an international audience. The photographic exhibit received hundreds of glowing written comments from visitors from around the world.

The tribute was also featured at The 1987 World Conference on Indigenous Peoples' Education at the University of British Columbia and at 30 other venues in Canada. Many public school classes have taken field trips specifically to view the show which is considered the first comprehensive work of its kind in Canada.

Proposing a Year of the Elder

The idea of a Year of the Elder came to me after seeing the impact the exhibit had at Expo '86 and realizing that Native Elders are genuinely cherished as the heart and core of their culture. This fact, contrasted with the rising cases of abuse against old people and increasing numbers of seniors in modern society — the age wave — prompted me to do some research for my proposal.

In 1988, in meetings with the United Nations, UN Association and UNESCO heads of Canada, the need for a Year of the Elder was proposed, recognizing the positive role that First Nations Elders could offer the rest of society. To advance the notion of a Year of the Elder, Canada's UN Association president David Cadman took a compact version of the photographic tribute on

a trip to Beijing and Moscow. While on tour, Cadman made presentations on behalf of *Our Elders Speak* and Year of the Elder to the Soviet and Chinese UN Association officials. In 1989 the World Headquarters of UNESCO in Paris endorsed *Our Elders Speak* as Project Number 322 which is now officially recognized as an Activity of the World Decade for Cultural Development. The exhibit has since been invited on an overseas tour to raise awareness of the importance of Elders.

To promote the project and rally support for a Year of the Elder, the non-profit Our Elders Speak Wisdom Society was officially incorporated on January 15, 1990. Founded by a cross-cultural team of First Nations Elders, professionals, and others, our mission is to bring the teachings of indigenous Elders into the public mainstream and focus global awareness on the wisdom, strengths, and power of age. Although the idea of a Year of the Elder is being entertained at many levels of society, an official declaration is still in the offing as of the first printing of this book.

The Global Need for Indigenous Wisdom

Indigenous Elders were speaking — and living — their wisdom of nature ages before environmental issues came into vogue. As Chief Joseph of the Nez Percé tribe said in 1890: "Myself and the Earth are of one mind."

More recently however, industrial and technological development has contaminated the natural environment and devastated indigenous peoples the world over. Our air and water is polluted. We are rapidly destroying our oxygen-producing, medicine-rich rainforests and in the name of progress we are bringing about the extinction of countless wildlife species which have been part of the intricate web of our eco-system for millions of years. The planet is sick. Scientists and environmentalists are warning us that we have less than 10 years to turn it around.

At the very core of the environmental crisis are the misconceptions and unhealthy attitudes toward nature and toward indigenous peoples. Our current problems may have begun when the first Europeans arrived in North America, thinking they were in India. Their attitude was that the aboriginal people had no more status than that of the plants and animals. They were of little consequence. The newcomers placed themselves hierarchically above the "Indians" and above nature. And when we place ourselves hierarchically above everything else we lose our place in nature and we lose our sense of humility. We have lost our respect for the equal rights of all living things. Nooksack's 98-year old tribal Elder Joe Louie affirmed: "It is true. Before Christianity was brought over here, we used to worship and respect everything."

There is a need for more than the recycling of materials and the reduction of pollution. There is a need for the re-awakening of respect for all living things. We have come to our logical end, which takes us back to the beginning in our circle of life, or in the words of Chief Seattle: "What we do to the Earth, we do to ourselves, because we are the Earth."

Perhaps there is no new solution to our environmental mess. Perhaps the solution is very old, yet alive and thriving in the hearts of our First People. Indigenous Elders must be seen and heard — they hold valuable secrets for humanity.

While the news media tends to focus on the confrontations, protests and stand-offs involving aboriginal people, this book celebrates the benevolent qualities of the Elders. It is more than a tribute to the Elders; it is a reflection of their teachings. While the definition of an Elder will vary from one group to the next, they traditionally were — and still are — teachers of time-tested values that are rooted in reverence for nature. It is not only the words of the Elders that teach; it is also their non-verbal warmth and kindness and humour that touches, teaches and heals.

Now is the time to listen and learn because our Elders speak from the heart of Creation.

Karie Garnier

Let's Celebrate
a World-wide
Year of
The Elder

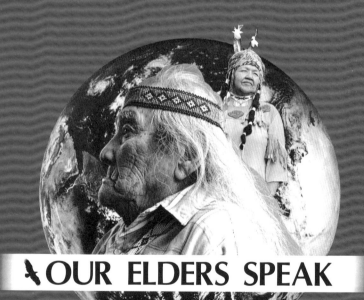

OUR ELDERS SPEAK

A Photographic Tribute

"Through ceremonies we help ourselves, help people, help Mother Earth."

Napoleon Kruger – Okanagan
Born 1923, Marron Valley, Penticton, B.C.

Napoleon Kruger is an Elder of the land. He is also a ceremonial pipe-holder and a drug and alcohol counsellor. Napoleon works with Native Medicines and travels extensively helping his people in traditional ways. He and his wife Elizabeth raised nine children and today enjoy their 26 grandchildren on their traditional land near Penticton, B.C. Napoleon Kruger is a spiritual adviser to *Our Elders Speak* project.

"We spend about a week on the mountain. Alone. Fasting and praying. That's where it all begins."

'Poncho' – Secwepemc
Born 1896, Chase, B.C.

Poncho or Harry Dick worked as a soldier during World War One, then as a federally commissioned policeman for 32 years in the Chase area. *Poncho*, a well-known Indian singer, was the son of a Medicine Man.

"Love the Mother Earth and she'll take care of you."

Rose Sparrow – Sto:lo
Born 1902, Chilliwack, B.C.

Rose married her husband Ed Sparrow when she was sixteen
years old. They lived on the Musqueam Reserve for seventy
years where they raised seven children. Rose Sparrow's family
now includes 39 grandchildren and 59 great grandchildren.
Rose was an accomplished traditional weaver and knitter.

"*Welcome to our land!*"

Ed Sparrow – Sto:lo
Born 1898, The Musqueam Reserve, Vancouver, B.C.

Ed Sparrow, Musqueam's eldest Elder is still very active as a fisherman and gardener. In his earlier days he was also a leader in the Native Brotherhood. Ed and his late wife Rose raised seven children on the Musqueam Reserve. Grampa Ed today is loved by his 39 grandchildren and 59 great grandchildren.

"My heart is real good today because all my life I loved helping old people."

Celina August – Sto:lo
Born 1916, The Musqueam Reserve, Vancouver, B.C.

The Musqueam People refer to Celina August as their Miracle Lady after her complete recovery from a totally paralyzing illness. When Celina was only ten years old she began shearing her grandmother's sheep and knitting Indian clothing. She has made thousands of Indian sweaters. Celina raised two daughters and has four grandchildren.

"Me? I'm just Molly."

Molly Campbell – Sto:lo
Born 1912, The Musqueam Reserve, Vancouver, B.C.

Molly Campbell raised six children on the Musqueam
Reserve where she still lives happily in the company of her 18
grandchildren and six great grandchildren.

"In my lifetime I've known all nationalities and found they are all good people."

Andy Natrall – Squamish
Born 1895, Squamish, B.C.

The Squamish people remember Andy as their living history book. He was an outstanding fisherman, a longshoreman, a soldier, and a logger. He was also a great hunter until his early 80s. Andy Natrall was familiar with Native Medicines and said he had never been sick nor had an enemy. Andy raised seven children on the Mission Reserve. More than 70 grandchildren and great grandchildren cherish the legacy of Andy Natrall.

"My door is always open."

Sadie Baker – Squamish
Born 1902, Cedar District, Vancouver Island, B.C.

Sadie Baker married and settled in Squamish where her late husband Sam Baker became an early member of the Indian Shaker Church. Sadie, a writer and poet, helped establish the Indian Homemakers' Club and over the decades has become mother to countless Indian children. Sadie Baker's adopted family now extends across North America.

"Be a brother to all."

Chief Alvie Andrew – Squamish
Born 1902, Squamish, B.C.

Alvie Andrew worked as a logger in the mountains around
Squamish, B.C. and was known for his practice of run-
ning barefoot several miles to work every morning. He
served his people of the upper Squamish Indian Band as
Chief-in-Council for 36 years and is the last of their
hereditary chiefs. Alvie raised five children and today enjoys
his 14 grand-children, 16 great grandchildren, and one great
great grandchild.

"Kindness pays dividends you'll never regret, so always be kind to others."

Emma Joe – Squamish
Born 1905, The Burrard Reserve, North Vancouver, B.C.

Emma Joe dedicated her life to working with native children – originally at the Native Indian Residential School in Kamloops, B.C. and later in her North Vancouver home as mother to eight of her own children and several orphans. Emma Joe's love still shines through her increasing family of grandchildren.

"Treat all people the way you want them to treat you."

Edward G. Nahanee – Squamish
Born 1897, Vancouver, B.C.

Edward Nahanee proudly described himself as a fighter for his
Native people. After working 33 years as a longshoreman,
Ed retired from the position of company superintendent in
1945. As business agent for the Native Brotherhood until
1973, he was politically active in legislating old age pensions
for Native Elders. Ed Nahanee also represented B.C. Native
fishermen on the International Salmon Commission. His home
was on the Mission Reserve in North Vancouver. Ed raised
12 children who have in turn provided Ed with more than 50
grandchildren and numerous great grandchildren.

"Fellowship, communication and working together is the strength of our Indian People."

Chief Simon Baker – Squamish
Born 1911, The Capilano Reserve, North Vancouver, B.C.

Simon Baker, a prominent Native leader, is internationally recognized as an ambassador for the First Nations of Canada. Simon worked for 40 years as a longshoreman and as a councillor of the Squamish Indian Band. Simon and his wife Emily raised nine children on the Capilano Reserve in North Vancouver. They have 27 grandchildren and 17 great grandchildren. Simon was elected King of Native Elders of British Columbia in 1989. In 1990 Chief Simon Baker received a Doctor of Laws degree from the University of British Columbia.

"If you haven't had a cup of tea or coffee with a Native Indian you don't know anything about us."

Minnie Croft – Haida
Born 1909, Haida Gwaii

Minnie Croft was born in the Queen Charlotte Islands where she later opened her own coffee shop. Since moving to Vancouver in 1932, she has also managed a Native craft store, a hotel, and worked voluntarily for almost every Native organization in the city. For six years Minnie Croft was president of the Vancouver local of the United Native Nations.

"I thank you Great Spirit for allowing us to call upon you in our times of need, asking you to bless these beloved people who walk in this world of your creation. Oh good Creator, help us all as we stand looking toward you in our own way."

Joe Washington – Lummi
Born 1919, The Lummi Reservation, Washington, U.S.A.

Joe's training in Native spirituality began, he explains, when a killer whale saved him from drowning in the Strait of Juan de Fuca. He was only a child at the time. The big 'blackfish' safely deposited young Joe on the sandy shore in front of his home. Joe dedicated the rest of his life to working for God. He and his wife raised five children on the Lummi Reservation and adopted a multitude of grandchildren. "I still know how to talk with the whales," says Joe Washington, "because they are my friends."

41

"All of Creation is sacred to indigenous people.   This is our message to the rest of the world."

Lavina White-Lightbown – Haida
Born 1921, Masset, Haida Gwaii

In 1976 Lavina became the first Native woman in Canada to be voted head of a Native nation. Lavina and her husband Bill raised seven children and are blessed with 15 grand-children and 10 great grand-children. Lavina and Bill now live in Vancouver. They remain actively dedicated to improving the situation of indigenous peoples.

"Love and respect for people and nature will bring you to the Great Spirit."

Lena Jacobs – Squamish
Born 1910, The Mission Reserve, North Vancouver, B.C.

Lena Jacobs worked for 30 years in a fish cannery in Vancouver. She and her husband also raised a family of eight children on the Capilano Reserve. Today Lena's grandchildren and great grandchildren number 27 and 32 respectively.

"Live a decent life. Get along with everybody. "

'Choppy' – **Lawrence James** – Sto:lo
Born 1897, The Skwah Reserve, Chilliwack, B.C.

Lawrence James was a musician, a canoe builder and an outstanding athlete. At an early age fellow lacrosse players nicknamed him *Choppy* because of his unique style with the lacrosse stick. *Choppy* was also a champion marathon runner and first place winner of the B.C. Indian Mile Race for five consecutive years. Lawrence James worked as a logger and raised a family of eight children in Chilliwack, B.C.

"Our Elders speak from the heart of this land."

Minnie Peters – Nlaka'pamux / Sto:lo
Born 1921, Spuzzum, B.C.

Minnie was born into the Nlaka'pamux Nation and later married into the Sto:lo Nation. Minnie and her husband Bob raised four of their own children, adopted one, and fostered many more on the Peters Reserve near Hope, B.C. Minnie is a director of the Indian Arts & Crafts Society of B.C. and is the founding vice-president of Our Elders Speak Wisdom Society. She tans hides, spins wool, knits sweaters, works with cedar bark, weaves blankets and rugs, designs and makes traditional Native clothing and shares her knowledge with young people.

"I've worked all my life and with all kinds of people. Come with me and I'll work with you too."

Willy George – Sto:lo
Born 1903, The Ohamil Reserve, Hope, B.C.

Willy George worked for most of his life as a logger and with
the Canadian National Railway. He raised six children near
Hope, B.C. and is warmly remembered by many grandchildren.

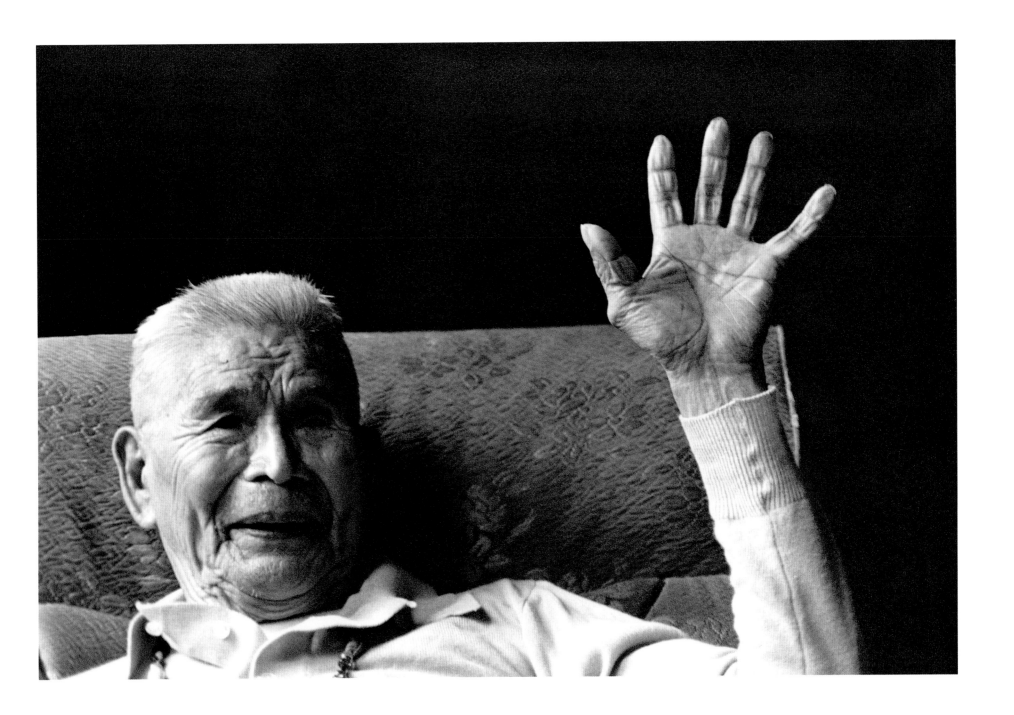

"When picking a plant for Indian Medicine, first we give an offering and an apology. Then we take only as much as we need."

Edna Bobb – Sto:lo
Born 1914, Chehalis, B.C.

Edna Bobb helped write the dictionary of her Halkemelem language and presently teaches school near her home at Seabird Island. Edna knows her people's history and understands natural Native Medicines. Edna raised three children and today enjoys her 14 grandchildren and nine great grandchildren.

"Don't smoke, don't drink and take care of your own business."

Mary Ferguson-Bessette – Cree
Born 1894, Northern Peace River, Alberta

As a young woman, Mary Ferguson was known as the best dress-maker in Northern Peace River. Mary and her husband worked in Notikewin, Alberta as fur traders, and later opened a general store there. In the late forties they retired and moved to the B.C. coast. Today Mary Ferguson-Bessette shares her large White Rock home with her grandchildren and great grandchildren who love to hear grandma play old tunes on her harmonica.

"Our people are coming back real strong – now that we've returned to our sharing and praying in the sweat lodge."

Nancy Phillips – Sto:lo
Born 1907, The Tzeachten Reserve, Sardis, B.C.

Nancy Phillips completed The Halkemelem Teacher's Training Program at Fraser Valley College and has been teaching the language for the past 17 years on her home reserve in Chehalis, B.C. Nancy and her husband had 12 children and today enjoy the company of their 36 grandchildren and 40 great grandchildren.

"What good is education without love?"

Catherine Adams – Kwakiutl
Born 1903, Smiths Inlet, B.C.

"I was born away up the coast, long before there were any gas boats," explains Catherine. "My mother nearly gave birth to me right in our dugout canoe – miles out in the strait." Fortunately, Catherine's father managed to paddle the canoe in the nick of time, to a tiny moss-covered islet. "I was born on a big rock," chuckles Catherine. When she was only a few hours old her ears were pierced – as they are today. In her early years she travelled the coast as a nurse on the mission boat *Columbia* servicing the Native communities. Later she helped establish the St. James Social Service in downtown Vancouver. Catherine and her husband Ralph now live in Port Hardy on Vancouver Island. Catherine Adams – a living legacy of the Kwakiutl Nation – is cherished by her great grandchildren.

"All living things understand you. And they will help you – if you respect them. This is the one thing we should never forget."

Joe Louie – Nooksack
Born 1892, Northwood, Washington, U.S.A.

The Coast Salish people recognize Joe Louie as a great hunter, provider, and as a man of the land. His personal knowledge of the seasonal movements of the animals and fish throughout northwest Washington has been permanently recorded in his illustrated land map of the area. Joe Louie's map, written in the Halkemelem language, depicts the major land masses, waterways and movements of wildlife in relation to Nooksack tribal history.

"When you see the eagle, say: 'Thank you Grandfather, thank you Grandmother for appearing today, for looking over me and for giving me strength'."

Mary Uslick – Secwepemc / Sto:lo
Born 1919, Kamloops, B.C.

Mary Uslick is a spiritual teacher and an active member of the Coqualeetza Elders' Group. At the age of 10 she was cured of a life-threatening illness by a traditional healer. She has since devoted more than 60 years to helping others through Native Medicines. Originally from the Secwepemc Nation in Kamloops, B.C., she married into the Sto:lo Nation in Sardis, B.C., in the 1940s. She has worked voluntarily within the prison system helping Native inmates who refer to her as "Mom". Mary has supported and given guidance to many organizations and is the recipient of the Fraser Valley Outstanding Woman Award. Mary Uslick is also an adviser and the founding president of Our Elders Speak Wisdom Society.

"To bring about the healing of an individual or a nation depends on respect for all things that have life including the rocks, the mountains and the waters. We should show our respect for all things and all people. And we should respect the differences. We call on the animals, the four-leggeds, the two-leggeds, the lightning, the thunder, the wind, the eagle – we call on all these spirits in order to attain these healing powers."

Rolling Thunder – Cherokee
Born 1916, Talihina, Oklahoma, U.S.A.

Rolling Thunder is a spiritual teacher and internationally respected traditional healer. He has travelled extensively on speaking tours and is the subject of the book *Rolling Thunder* by Doug Boyd of the Menninger Foundation. He made his home in Carlin, Nevada and also worked on the Southern & Pacific Railway for 36 years. Rolling Thunder explains that, as a healer, he does nothing because all power belongs to the Great Spirit. Rolling Thunder has been instrumental in the healing of numerous individuals including the author of *Our Elders Speak – A Tribute To Native Elders.*

Rolling Thunder with a wild Golden Eagle

"The Grandmothers and Grandfathers will help you."

Standing Eagle – Okanagan

Sunset at the 1987 Stein Festival

The Hopi Prophet Thomas Banyacya

Nis'ga Nation Elder Lucy Williams

Sorting wild berries

Colouring a picture for . . .

Elder Alfred Racelma

Napoleon in communion with the mountains – Stein Valley, 1985

A Bald Eagle soars

Kwakiutl Elders: Jimmy Sewid; Willie Hunt; Alvin Alfred

Albert Lightning, Elder of the Cree Nation

Katie Adams speaks at her 1986 potlatch

Button blankets and babies

Elder Willy George of the Sto:lo Nation

Elder Eva Lewis and great grandson

In full regalia and in good spirits

Working hands are happy hands

Native children of many nations

Caucasian child with Maori Elder

Our Medicine People love Laughter

Adeline Point with grandaughter

Sunshine

Through

Memories

of

the

Late

Rose

Sparrow

ABOUT VOLUME ONE

This first publication celebrates a few of the Native Elders from the Pacific Northwest. To properly pay tribute to the Elders of all Native Nations would require many volumes. Volume One is a beginning.

Reflecting back over this nine-year journey with the Elders, many wonderful experiences come to mind. A truly unforgettable incident is captured in the photograph (page 65) of Rolling Thunder holding the Golden Eagle. When we first approached the great wild bird on Rolling Thunder's land in the Nevada desert, it was on the alert, its beak opened — as if ready to strike.

Without hesitating, Rolling Thunder moved his opened steady hand directly up to its sharp bill. The bird did not move. Rolling Thunder then, very slowly, stroked its head feathers — three times. "Now," explained Rolling Thunder, "anyone can pet this eagle. After this it'll be tamer than a chicken."

The Golden Eagle stayed for seven months and then he set it free.

With the blessings of the Elders, more anecdotes, Elders' statements and other stories will get published in a subsequent volume.

*   *   *

ACKNOWLEDGEMENTS

Although the many people who actively supported this project are far too numerous to list on a single page, the nine years of work resulting in this publication was made possible with the assistance of the following individuals and groups:

Chief Leonard George and the Chief Dan George Memorial Foundation; the Canada Council Explorations Program; the Department of the Secretary of State of Canada and their former Senior Officer of Native Programs, Cheryl Brooks; Gloria Nicolson and the Professional Native Womens' Association; the Van Dusen Foundation; the Vancouver Centennial Commission; Esso Resources; WC^2; Our Elders Speak Wisdom Society; the individual Elders, Elders Groups, Elders' coordinators, administrators and staff at the Coqualeetza Education Training Centre; the Musqueam Band; the Squamish Band; and other bands; the ongoing guidance of Rolling Thunder, Mary Uslick, Napoleon Kruger and family; and most important of all — the one Elder, nurturer, and life-giver constantly behind this project with a heart — my friend and mother, Ferne.

Paul George and Jim Astell offered important suggestions for the book; Preston Denny helped refine the graphic design; Lorna Williams, Adeline Saunders and Carlyn Yandle helped review the text for errors. Perry Boeker and the staff at Hemlock Printers were helpful beyond the call of duty. Any remaining inaccuracies or omissions are, of course the responsibility of the author.

David Cadman and the United Nations Association of Canada contributed generously toward the first printing.

And to the true friends and everybody who has given encouragement over many years, it is all of you — whose names are not mentioned — who are also in this work. Thank you. The spirit of your friendship has helped to keep this project alive.

The photographs were taken with a SLR 35mm Canon camera,
50mm f 1.8 lens, Soligor 2x teleconverter, and 400 ASA black and white film using available natural lighting.

This book is printed on high quality, acid free paper
TO LAST FOR GENERATIONS TO COME.

IN GRATITUDE

I am deeply grateful to all our consistently warm-hearted Native Elders, their families and the Elders' coordinators who have so generously supported and participated in this work. In the process, my circle of family and friends has naturally grown to embrace the Native community. I feel greatly enriched and share the prayer of the Native Elders that the good feelings generated through their images and quotations will help uplift all people.

Karie Garnier

"Hard work will keep you alive and well."

Margaret White – Cree
Born 1917, The Erminskin Reserve, Hobbema, Alberta

"Caring and sharing is a big part of our Indian way."

Wilfred Charlie – Sto:lo
Born 1917, Blaine, Washington, U.S.A.